Sachin Tendulkar

www.pegasusforkids.com

© **B. Jain Publishers (P) Ltd.** All rights reserved. No part of this book may be reproduced, stored in a retrieval system or transmitted, in any form or by any means, mechanical, photocopying, recording or otherwise, without any prior written permission of the publisher.

Published by Kuldeep Jain for B. Jain Publishers (P) Ltd., D-157, Sector 63, Noida - 201307, U.P
Registered office: 1921/10, Chuna Mandi, Paharganj, New Delhi-110055

Printed in India

Contents

- **5** Who is Sachin Tendulkar?
- **6** Childhood Years and Introduction to Cricket
- **16** Sachin in His Growing-Up Years
- **19** Career at Home
- **24** Global Career
- **38** Achievements
- **46** Sachin and Anjali
- **50** Sachin—the Man
- **52** Retirement
- **55** Timeline
- **59** Activities
- **62** Glossary

Who is Sachin Tendulkar?

When Sachin Tendulkar made his test debut against Pakistan as a 16-year-old, little did the world know that the curly haired teenager would one day become one of the greatest legends of the game! Tendulkar is more than just a popular sportsperson; he is an institution in himself. He is not just loved and respected, but revered by all. Called the God of Cricket by his fans, Tendulkar has ruled the game for well over two decades—a very rare feat for a sportsperson. Widely considered to be the greatest cricketer ever, he is the only player to have scored one hundred international centuries.

Regarded as one of the greatest batsmen ever, Sachin Ramesh Tendulkar is the foundation of Indian batting for more than two decades. He is the world's leading run-scorer in both Test (15,921) and ODI (18,426) cricket. In 2011, Tendulkar achieved his dream of winning the Cricket World Cup at the Wankhede stadium in Mumbai. It took six World Cup appearances for the 'Little Master' to be part of the team that won the coveted trophy.

Tendulkar has been the leading century maker in both Test and ODI, and has to his credit 100 (51 Test + 49 ODI) international centuries. He has been the most complete batsman of his time, the most prolific run-maker of all times, and arguably the biggest cricket icon the game has ever known.

Childhood Years and Introduction to Cricket

Tendulkar was born on April 24, 1973 at Nirmal Nursing Home in Mumbai, Maharashtra, India. His father, Ramesh Tendulkar, was a well-known Marathi novelist and his mother, Rajni, worked in the insurance industry. Sachin was named after his father's favourite music director, Sachin Dev Burman. Tendulkar has three elder siblings; two half-brothers Nitin and Ajit, and a half-sister Savita. They are from his father's first marriage.

Young Sachin spent his formative years in the Sahitya Sahawas Cooperative Housing Society in Bandra (East), Mumbai. As a young boy, Tendulkar was considered a bully. He often picked up fights with new children in his school. To help curb his mischievous and bullying tendencies, Ajit, his elder brother, introduced him to cricket in 1984. He introduced young Sachin to Ramakant Achrekar, a famous cricket coach and a club cricketer of standing, at Shivaji Park, Dadar, Mumbai.

When young Sachin met Achrekar for the first time, he did not play his best. Ajit told Achrekar that Sachin was feeling self-conscious due to the coach observing him, and was not displaying his natural game. Ajit requested the coach to give him another chance at playing, but watch while hiding behind a tree. This time Sachin, apparently unobserved, played much better and was accepted at Achrekar's academy. Ajit is 10 years older, and is credited by Sachin for playing a pivotal role in his life.

Coach Achrekar was impressed with Tendulkar's talent and advised him to shift his schooling to Sharadashram Vidyamandir (English) High School, a school at Dadar Mumbai, which had a leading cricket team and had produced many notable cricketers. Before this, Tendulkar had attended the Indian Education Society's New English School in Bandra (East) Mumbai. He was also coached under the guidance of Achrekar at Shivaji Park in the mornings and evenings. Tendulkar would practise for hours. When he became exhausted, Achrekar would put a one-rupee coin on the top of the stumps, and the bowler who dismissed Tendulkar would get the coin. If Tendulkar passed the whole session without getting dismissed,

the coach would give him the coin. To win the coin, a tired Tendulkar needed to put a huge concentration in his batting. In this way, Tendulkar won thirteen coins and he treasured them. So, from there, Sachin got the

base of playing many long innings in both international and domestic cricket. In the present times, Tendulkar considers those 13 coins he won then as some of his most prized possessions.

Achrekar himself played for a long time in the local league of Mumbai. However, he could never make it big. Nevertheless, he had a great technique of the game and was regarded as a good cricketer in Mumbai. Achrekar had a great impact on Tendulkar and is credited for his coaching the little master and his success in international cricket.

Achrekar took Tendulkar to different fields of Mumbai and made him play against and for different clubs. This practice made Tendulkar habituated to cope up with different conditions very quickly from his childhood. He got various chances to play lots of matches in his childhood due to Achrekar's initiatives. Most of the time, Achrekar made Tendulkar play against older and comparatively experienced players both in the net and matches. Hence, Tendulkar got a great exposure and prepared himself for playing for the bigger stage from an early age. Achrekar

wanted Tendulkar to be in cricket as much as possible and encouraged him to work very hard.

At school, Tendulkar developed a reputation of a child prodigy. He had become a common conversation point in local cricketing circles, where people already suggested that he would become one of the greatest cricketers that India has ever produced. Tendulkar consistently featured in his school Shardashram Vidyamandir team in the Matunga Gujarati Seva Mandal (popularly coined MGSM) Shield. Besides school cricket, he also played club cricket, initially representing John Bright Cricket Club in

Mumbai's premier club cricket tournament, the Kanga League. Later, he went on to play for the Cricket Club of India.

In 1987, at the age of 14, he attended the MRF Pace Foundation in Chennai to be trained as a fast bowler. But the Australian fast bowler Dennis Lillee, who took a record 355 Test wickets, was unimpressed by Tendulkar. He suggested that Tendulkar should focus on his batting instead. On January 20, 1987, Sachin became the substitute for Imran Khan's side in an exhibition game at Brabourne

Stadium in Mumbai, to mark the golden jubilee of Cricket Club of India. A couple of months later, former Indian batsman Sunil Gavaskar gave him a pair of his own ultra-light pads and consoled him to not get dismayed for not getting the Mumbai Cricket Association's 'Best Junior Cricket Award'. He was 14 years that time. "It was the greatest source of encouragement for me," Tendulkar said nearly 20 years later after surpassing Gavaskar's world record of 34 Test centuries.

Sachin in His Growing-Up Years

Looking back at his childhood, Tendulkar was always a naughty child; his friends remember him climbing mango trees to pluck mangoes for them. They all used to wait for the little master to throw the fruits towards them.

His family members used to worry about Tendulkar's future. However, his elder brother, Ajit Tendulkar, ensured that his little brother had a great future, by recognizing his talent and introducing Sachin to the world of cricket at a very young age.

In school, Tendulkar was notorious for picking up fights with children who had come there for the first time and this led him to be regarded as a bully amidst his mates.

In his teens, Tendulkar was a great admirer of John McEnroe, one of the prominent tennis stars from the US who was also known for his fits of temper. Tendulkar's

brother, however, felt that Sachin should overcome his bullying and mischievous nature and so he introduced Sachin to cricket in 1984. It was at this time that Ajit took Sachin to Ramakant Achrekar, who was one of the most well-known club cricketers of his time as well as a top coach.

Career at Home

In the year 1987, on November 14, Tendulkar was selected to represent Mumbai in the Ranji Trophy, India's leading domestic first-class cricket tournament, for the 1987–88 season. However, he failed to get selected for the final eleven in any of the matches, although he was often used as a substitute fielder.

A year later, on December 11, 1988, when he was 15 years old, Tendulkar made his debut for Mumbai against Gujarat at home and scored 100-not-out in that match. This match made him the youngest Indian to score a century on debut in first-class cricket. He was handpicked to play for the team by the then Mumbai Captain Dilip Vengsarkar after watching him easily negotiating India's best fast bowler at the time, Kapil Dev, in the Wankhede Stadium nets, where the Indian team had come to play

against the touring New Zealand team. Sachin followed this by scoring a century in his first Deodhar and Duleep Trophies, the Indian domestic tournaments.

Tendulkar finished the 1988–89 season as Mumbai's highest run-scorer. He also made an unbeaten century in the Irani Trophy match against Delhi at the beginning of the 1989–90 season, playing for the rest of India. At this time, Tendulkar was picked for a young Indian team to tour England twice, under the Star Cricket Club banner

in 1988 and 1989. In the famous 1990–91 Ranji Trophy final, in which Haryana defeated Mumbai by two runs after leading in the first innings, Tendulkar's 96 from 75 deliveries was a key to giving Mumbai a chance of victory on the final day.

Tendulkar is the only player to score a century on debut in all three of his domestic first-class tournaments (the Ranji, Irani, and Duleep Trophies). Another double century was in an innings against Tamil Nadu in the semi-finals of the

2000 Ranji Trophy, which he regards as one of the best innings of his career!

In 1992, at the age of 19, Tendulkar became the first overseas-born player to represent Yorkshire which, prior to Tendulkar joining the team, had never before selected players even from other English counties. Selected for Yorkshire as a replacement for the injured Australian fast bowler Craig McDermott, Tendulkar played 16 first-class matches for the county and scored 1070 runs.

Global Career

Tendulkar's first exposure to international cricket came when he appeared as a substitute for Imran Khan's team at an exhibition game that was being staged at the Brabourne Stadium in Mumbai. The game was being played as a commemoration of the golden jubilee of CCI where Tendulkar used to play. In India's match against England during the semi-final of the 1987 World Cup in Mumbai, Tendulkar played the role of a ball-boy.

Tendulkar had an exceptional season in 1988 and scored a century in every match that he played. With his former friend and team India colleague Vinod Kambli, he took part in an unbeaten partnership of 664 runs against St. Xavier's High School in a Lord Harris Shield interschool contest. Their dominance was such that the opposition was not keen on going ahead with the match. Tendulkar notched up a 326 in that particular match and also scored in excess of 1000 runs in the tournament. His partnership was to stay unbroken till 2006 when a couple of under-13 batsmen eclipsed it at a game held in Hyderabad.

The proverb 'morning shows the day' was proven true for

Tendulkar. With sheer diligence and hard work, along with unfathomable natural talent, the young cricketer demonstrated the qualities that propelled him to win a place in the national team at the tender age of 16. He played against Pakistan, which was one of the toughest teams to play against at that time! Tendulkar performed brilliantly during that tour and the rest as they say is history!

Early Years

It is Raj Singh Dungarpur who is credited with the selection of Tendulkar for the Indian tour of Pakistan in late 1989. The Indian selection committee had shown interest in selecting Tendulkar for the tour of the West Indies held earlier that year, but eventually did not select

him, as they did not want him to be exposed to the dominant fast bowlers of the West Indies so early in his career. Tendulkar made his Test debut against Pakistan in Karachi in November 1989; he was just 16 years of age then. He managed to score only 15 runs, being bowled out by Waqar Younis, who was also making his debut in that match. In the fourth and final Test in Sialkot, Tendulkar was hit on the nose by a bouncer bowled by

Younis, but he declined medical assistance and continued to bat even as he bled profusely. In a 20-over exhibition game in Peshawar, held in parallel with the bilateral series, Tendulkar made 53 runs out of 18 balls, including an over in which he scored 27 runs off leg-spinner Abdul Qadir. This was later called 'one of the best innings I have seen' by the then Indian captain Krishnamachari Srikkanth. In all, Tendulkar scored 215 runs at an average of 35.83 in the Test series.

Hence, at 16, Tendulkar became the youngest player to debut for India in both Tests and ODIs.

The series was followed by a tour of New Zealand in which he scored 117 runs at an average of 29.25 in Tests, including an innings of 88 in the second Test. On his next tour to England in July-August 1990, he became the second youngest cricketer to score a Test century as he made 119* in the second Test at Old Trafford in Manchester. Wisden Cricketers' Almanack described his innings as 'a disciplined display of immense maturity.'

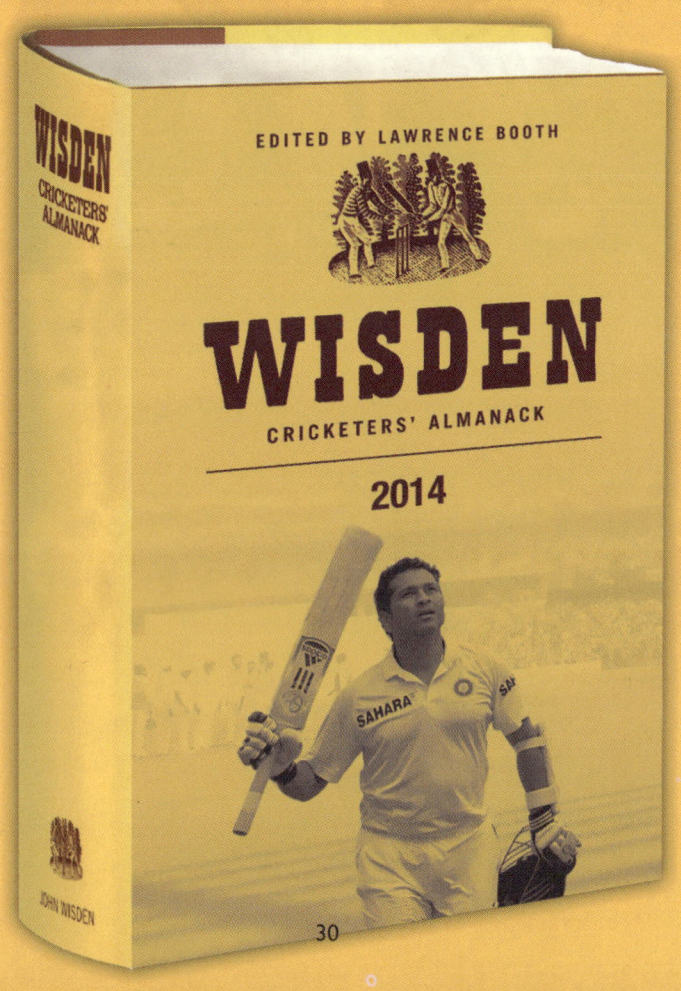

Tendulkar's performance through the years 1994–1999 coincided with his physical peak, in his early twenties. On the day of the Hindu festival Holi, Tendulkar was told to open the batting at Auckland against New Zealand in 1994. He went on to score 82 runs off 49 balls. He scored his first ODI century on September 9, 1994, against Australia in Colombo.

Tendulkar continued to shine and rise in his career when he became the leading run scorer at the 1996 World Cup, scoring two centuries. He was the only Indian batsman to perform remarkably well in the semi-final against Sri Lanka.

After the World Cup, in the same year against Pakistan at Sharjah, Indian captain Mohammed Azharuddin was going through a lean patch. Tendulkar and Navjot Singh Sidhu both made centuries to set a record partnership for the second wicket in the match. After getting out, Tendulkar found Azharuddin hesitant about whether he should bat or not. Tendulkar convinced him to bat and Azharuddin subsequently unleashed 24 runs off just one over. India went on to win the match at a great margin and the match enabled India to post a score in excess of 300 runs for the first time in an ODI.

This was the beginning of a golden period in the cricketing world. During the Australian tour of India in early 1998, Tendulkar scored three consecutive centuries. During the match, the entire focus lay on the clash between Tendulkar, the world's then most dominating batsman, and Shane Warne, the world's leading spinner, both of whom were at the peak of their careers. They were clashing in a full-fledged Test series after 7 long years. Tendulkar made an unbeaten 204 as Shane Warne conceded 111 runs in 16 overs and Australia lost the match within three days.

In the year 1999, the inaugural Asian Test Championship took place in February and March. Held just twice, the 1999 championship was contested by India, Pakistan and Sri Lanka. The first Test match between India and Pakistan in Eden Gardens was previously scheduled as the third Test match of the tournament. However, later on, it was shifted to be played as the first match. In the first match,

Tendulkar was run out for 9 after colliding with Pakistan bowler Shoaib Akhtar. Around 100,000 spectators came to support team India during the initial four days of the tournament. The aggregate Test attendance record, which was made 63 years ago, was broken during this Test. So agitated was the crowd at Tendulkar's dismissal that it started hurling objects at Akhtar, as a result of which the players were taken off the field.

The match resumed after Tendulkar and the president of the ICC appealed to the crowd. However, further rioting meant that the match was finished in front of a crowd of just 200 people. Tendulkar scored his 19th Test century in the second Test and the match resulted in a draw with Sri Lanka. India did not progress to the final, which was won by Pakistan, and refused to participate the next time the championship was held due to increasing political tensions between India and Pakistan.

In the historic Test match against Pakistan at Chepauk in 1999, the first of a two-Test series, Tendulkar scored 136 in the fourth innings with India chasing 271 for victory. However, he was knocked out when India needed just 17 more runs to win, triggering a batting collapse, and India lost the match by 12 runs. The worst happened when Professor Ramesh Tendulkar, his father, passed away while Tendulkar was in the middle of the 1999 Cricket World Cup. Tendulkar flew back to India to attend the last rites of his father, missing the match against Zimbabwe. However, he returned to the World Cup scoring a century (140 not out off 101 balls) in his very next

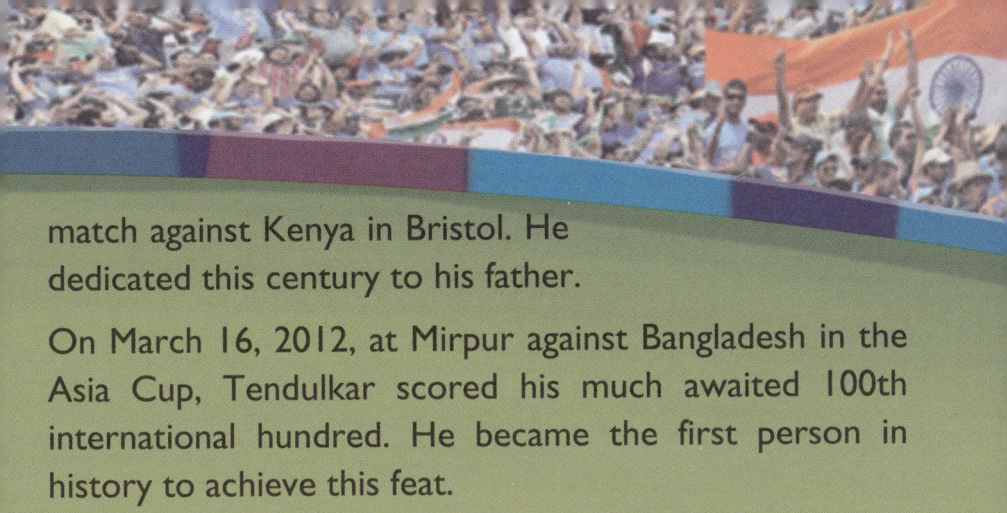

match against Kenya in Bristol. He dedicated this century to his father.

On March 16, 2012, at Mirpur against Bangladesh in the Asia Cup, Tendulkar scored his much awaited 100th international hundred. He became the first person in history to achieve this feat.

Achievements

Tendulkar is a remarkable cricketer whose talent and dedication is universally acclaimed. He has received India's highest sporting honour—the Rajiv Gandhi Khel Ratna—for 1997-1998, and the civilian awards Padma Shri in 1999 and Padma Vibhushan in 2008.

He is the leading run scorer in Tests, with 15,921 runs, as well as in One-Day Internationals, with 18,426 runs. He is the only player to score more than 30,000 runs in all forms of international cricket (Tests, ODIs and Twenty20 Internationals). He is the 16th player and the first Indian to score 50,000 runs in all forms of domestic and international recognized cricket (First-class, List A

and Twenty20). He achieved this feat on October 5, 2013, during a Champions League Twenty20 match for his IPL team 'Mumbai Indians' against Trinidad and Tobago.

He also holds the record for the highest number of centuries in both Tests and ODIs. On March 16, 2012, Tendulkar scored his 100th international hundred. It came against Bangladesh in the league matches of Asia Cup 2012.

Tendulkar has been part of most wins by an Indian in both Test cricket (72 wins) and ODIs (234 wins). He ranks third in the world in ODI victories after Ricky Ponting and Mahela Jayawardene. In fact, Tendulkar is the first batsman to score a double-century in one-day cricket.

ODI CAREER IN NUMBERS

463 MATCHES

18,426 RUNS IN ODI

200* HIGHEST SCORE

44.83 AVERAGE

49 HUNDREDS

96 FIFTIES

He has been 'Man of the Match' 13 times in Test matches and Man of the Series four times, two of them being for the Border-Gavaskar Trophy against Australia. His performance earned him respect from both Australian cricket fans and players. He has been 'Man of the Match' 62 times in One day International matches and 'Man of the Series' 15 times.

Tendulkar has consistently performed brilliantly in Cricket World Cups. He was the highest run scorer in the 1996 Cricket World Cup with a total of 523 runs and also of the 2003 Cricket World Cup with 673 runs. After his century against England during group stages of 2011 Cricket World Cup, he became the only player to

hit most number of centuries in Cricket World Cups with six centuries and the first player to score 2000 runs in World Cup cricket.

Tendulkar, the brightest star in the world of cricket, once said, "From the age of three, I've loved this sport and I've never thought about scoring the most number of centuries or runs in international cricket. Everyone enjoys breaking records, I'm enjoying it too, but that is not the reason for playing cricket."

On another occasion he said, "Whatever level you reach, getting better never stops." These words best define Tendulkar's principles and way of life.

Sachin and Anjali

Though Tendulkar has always been in the limelight due to his brilliance in the game, he prefers to have privacy in his personal life. He does not like to speak about his family in public. Although he did not speak much about his family in public, he never spared a chance to acknowledge their importance in his life.

Tendulkar got married to Anjali Mehta, the daughter of industrialist Ashok Mehta, in 1995. Anjali is of Gujarati descent and is a certified doctor by profession. The two

first met in 1990 at the Mumbai airport when Tendulkar was returning from his first tour of England and Anjali was there to pick up her mother.

Tendulkar and Anjali dated for a while before they tied the knot with the blessings of both the families. Today, the two are blessed with two kids, Arjun Tendulkar and Sarah Tendulkar.

"We had a courtship of five years and got married in 1995," stated Anjali, in a published interview. Anjali is a few years older than Tendulkar and is a paediatrician working at the JJ Hospital in Mumbai. She once said, "He hasn't spent Diwali at home since we got married. But it really doesn't matter that it's Diwali ... any time he spends at home is great!" These words of Anjali only reveal the warmth of their relationship.

Anjali once narrated an interesting incident when Tendulkar used a disguise to meet her. In the words of Anjali:

> *We had gone to see the movie Roja. I was studying medicine then and a couple of my friends planned it. Sachin did try telling me that it would be difficult, but I insisted that he come along. To make sure nobody recognised him, we even got him a beard. He wore specs as well and we went in late. We watched the first half of the film, but during the interval Sachin dropped his specs and people immediately acknowledged him! It was a bit of a disaster and we were forced to leave halfway.*

Anjali admits that she knew nothing about cricket when she first met Tendulkar. However, she read everything she could to learn more about the game. Tendulkar, on his part, does not discuss cricket at home. When at home, he loves listening to music and tries to spend every available hour indulging in it.

Sachin—the Man

From what is known of Tendulkar from his childhood days, he possessed an extraordinary talent for the game of cricket. Even into his late 30s, he practised as hard as he did when he was a teen. He knew that being complacent would lead to wastage of his natural gifts.

Although Tendulkar never said it in many words, but it was pretty obvious that he wanted to be the best in the world. All his efforts were directed towards achieving this remarkable goal.

Tendulkar, with all the talent and hype around him right from his teens, could have turned harsh and arrogant but he had the maturity to remain grounded even in fame!

It is widely believed that no one can achieve success without the support of other individuals. Even in Tendulkar's case, he had many who supported him through all phases of his life. Tendulkar, on his part, has also left no opportunity to show his gratefulness to all those people. During his farewell speech before retiring from the game of cricket, he made sure not to forget to thank anyone who had been kind to him.

Retirement

Tendulkar announced his retirement from One Day Internationals on December 23, 2012, while noting that he will be available for Test cricket.

On October 10, 2013, Tendulkar announced that he would retire from all formats of the game after the two-Test series against West Indies in November.

Later, the BCCI confirmed that the two matches would be played at Kolkata and Mumbai, ensuring the farewell took place on his home ground on Tendulkar's request. He scored 74 runs in his last Test innings against West Indies, falling short by 79 runs to complete 16,000 runs in Test cricket. The Cricket Association of Bengal and the Mumbai Cricket Association organized events to mark his retirement from the sport. Various national and international figures from cricket, politics, Bollywood and other fields spoke about him in a day-long 'Salaam Sachin Conclave' organized by India Today.

In July 2014, he led the MCC side in the Bicentenary Celebration match at Lord's. In December 2014, he was announced the ambassador of the ICC Cricket World Cup 2015 event. This marked his second term as he had already been held the ambassador of the previous ICC Cricket World Cup 2011.

Tendulkar's retirement leaves a huge void in the lives of his millions of fans.

In a career spanning almost 24 glorious and extraordinary years, Tendulkar has captured the imagination of millions and is a figure beyond the boundaries of the cricket field. Such is his following and fanfare that he could bring a country to a standstill with the magic of his performance.

Timeline

- **1973** Tendulkar is born on April 24, in Mumbai
- **1988** he scores 100 not out in his first first-class match for Bombay against Gujarat in the Ranji Trophy; he becomes the youngest cricketer to score a century on his first-class debut, aged 15 years
- **1989** he makes Test debut for India against Pakistan in Karachi at the age of 16

   he makes his debut in ODI against Pakistan but is dismissed by Waqar Younis without scoring a run
- **1990** he scores a maiden Test century against England at Old Trafford
- **1992** at the age of 19, Tendulkar becomes the first overseas-born player to represent Yorkshire
- **1994** he claims his first ODI century against Sri Lanka in Colombo after 79 one-day matches
- **1996** Tendulkar becomes the leading run scorer at World Cup played in India, Pakistan and Sri Lanka with a total of 523 runs

   he takes on the Indian captaincy although he suffers two relatively unsuccessful

Timeline

stints during a four-year period, winning only four Tests and 23 ODIs

- 1997 he earns the title of Wisden Cricketer of the Year

- 1998 he scores his first double century for Mumbai against Australia in the Brabourne Stadium

- 1999 he gets involved in India's highest run-scoring ODI partnership with Rahul Dravid as the pair put on 339 against New Zealand. In the same match, he records the highest individual ODI score in Indian history with an unbeaten 186

- 2000 he gives up the captaincy of Indian team after the two-Test series with South Africa

- 2003 he is named the Player of the Tournament at the 2003 Cricket World Cup; he scores 673 runs, the highest by any player in the tournament

- 2005 he broke Sunil Gavaskar's record of the highest number of Test centuries by claiming his 35th against Sri Lanka in Delhi

- **2006** he overtakes Kapil Dev claiming the record for the highest amount of Test appearances for India with 135

- **2007** he edges past Brian Lara's world record of runs scored in Tests away from home with 5,751 runs

    he becomes the first player to score over 15,000 ODI runs during a match against South Africa in Belfast

- **2008** he plays a record-breaking 417th ODI match against Australia

    he becomes the third player in Test match history, and the first from India, to play 150 matches when he is selected for the third Test against Sri Lanka

    he is nominated as the 'Icon Player' of IPL franchise Mumbai Indians, signing a deal worth US$ 1,121,250 per season

    he becomes the highest run scorer in Test cricket, passing Lara's previous mark of 11,953, when he reaches 16 in the first innings of the second Test against Australia

- **2010** he scores the first double century in one-day international history, hitting an unbeaten 200 against South Africa

Timeline

he is named player of IPL3 after finishing as the tournament's top run-scorer

he becomes the most capped player in Test history, making his 169th Test appearance in the third Test against Sri Lanka in Colombo to overtake former Australia captain Steve Waugh

he becomes the first batsman to hit 50 Test centuries

- 2011 he hits two tournament centuries as India wins the World Cup

  he becomes the first man to score 15,000 Test runs during the Test series against West Indies

- 2012 he scores his 100th international century in an Asia Cup match against Bangladesh, the first player ever to do so

  he announces retirement from one-day international cricket

- 2013 he announces retirement from Test cricket after playing his 200th Test against the West Indies in November

Project Work

Search the Internet or look up in encyclopaedias to collect information on any sport of your choice. Make a project on it. You may cover the following aspects:

- How the game is played
- Rules for playing the game
- Things required for playing the game
- Who are the stalwarts of the game

Do not forget to paste pictures for all the topics that you cover.

Outdoor Activity

Organize a game of cricket. Divide your class into two teams. Tell your class teacher to get the children trained by the sports teacher. You may call upon your school Principal to see the match. Do a bit of research about the rules of the game before you start playing.

Activities

Activities

Questions

1. Who is Sachin Tendulkar?
2. Why is he remarkable?
3. When and where was he born?
4. Name his parents.
5. Name the school which Sachin joined later due to their powerful cricket team.
6. Name Sachin's brother who actually introduced him to cricket.
7. Name the coach who trained Sachin in cricket in the initial stages of his life.
8. How did his coach motivate Sachin to practice more when he would get tired?
9. How did his coach give Sachin the exposure so that he could face all types of cricket?
10. Why did everyone think that he was a 'child prodigy'?
11. Describe Sachin as a child.
12. Which year did Sachin start playing for Ranji trophy?
13. Which tournament is considered to be Sachin's first exposure to international cricket?

14. List out some of the qualities of Sachin as an immensely successful cricketer.
15. How did Wisden Cricketers' Almanack describe Sachin?
16. How many ODIs and Test matches did Sachin play in his illustrious career?
17. Name some of the remarkable awards that Sachin won in his career.
18. Whom did Sachin marry? Where did they meet?
19. When did Sachin retire from cricket?
20. What was the reaction of his fans?

Activities

Glossary

acquit: to become free from a criminal charge

bilateral: something relating to two sides

bully: a person who uses strength to harm or frighten those who are weaker

coincide: to occur at the same time

commemoration: the action of commemorating a dead person or past event

consoled: to give comfort to someone in times of grief

decades: a period of 10 years

demonstrate: to clearly show the existence or truth of something by giving evidence

diligence: persistent in work or effort

disguise: to give a different look to a person to hide the original identity

dismissed: to order or allow someone to leave

domestic cricket: cricket that is played at home

efforts: a vigorous attempt in some work

encouraged: to give support and confidence

exceptional: unusual, not common

exhausted: to be very tired

Glossary

exhibition: a public display of works of art or items of interest

foundation: the lowest part of a building below ground

gratefulness: showing appreciation for something done

industrialist: a person who owns one or more industries

innings: in the game of cricket, each of the two or four divisions of a game during which one side has a turn at batting

insurance industry: an industry with companies which provide a guarantee of compensation for specified loss, damage, illness, or death in return for payment of a specified premium

legends: an extremely famous, especially in a particular field.

limelight: the focus of public attention

ODI: short form of 'one day international'

reputation: the opinions that are generally held about someone or something

requested: to ask politely or formally for something

Glossary

substitute: a person or thing serving in place of another

technique: the method of doing some particular work

teenager: a person aged between 13 and 19 years

tournament: a series of contests between a number of competitors for a common prize

unfathomable: something that cannot be explored

unobserved: not being observed